Get the Message!
Helen Astley

This book is about some of the ways in which messages are sent and received, in other words, about *communication*.

Our ability to communicate is the most important tool we have, and the more we understand about language and communication, the better we can use this tool.

We send messages not only by what we say but by the look on our faces, the way we move our bodies, through music and dance, and by using signs and signals. Sometimes we do not even realise we are communicating. In this book you will find out some of the different ways in which we communicate without words:

1. **Animal communication**

2. **Human communication without words**

3. **Signals and signs**

4. **Symbols**

5. **Made-up languages**

6. **Computers, codes and communication**

At the end you will be asked '*What do you think?*'

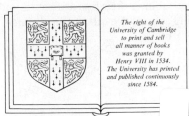

The right of the
University of Cambridge
to print and sell
all manner of books
was granted by
Henry VIII in 1534.
The University has printed
and published continuously
since 1584.

CAMBRIDGE

Cambridge
London   New Y
Melbourne   Syd

GW00569898

1 Animal communication

Humans are not the only creatures to communicate. If you have a pet, a cat or a dog, for example, you will probably know a great deal about how it communicates with you and with other animals. Communication is as important to animals as it is to us; without the ability to communicate they could not survive.

They need to communicate in order to mate and often to find food, to mark out territory, to warn of danger and to make clear their position in the group to avoid fighting. Animals have their own 'language', using *sound, scent, sight* and even *touch* signals.

Sound signals

S P

Many animals, like us, communicate with sound. Can you think of any? We have a number of words to describe the noises they make. See if you can find an animal to match each word in the list below:

bark, bleat, crow, neigh, roar, sing, squeak, croak, chatter, cluck, snort

Now try to find some more pairs of noises and animals.

Birds sing to attract a mate and to warn other birds off their territory (which may be a garden, a tree or just a branch). Different songs send different messages. Hens *cluck* all the time to reassure one another that they are safe; when danger threatens they give a *squawk* of alarm.

Crickets, grasshoppers, cicadas and locusts cannot sing but they do make sound by rubbing their legs against the sides of their body to make a chirping sound. We call this *stridulation*.

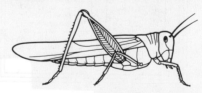

Did you know that even fish use sound to communicate? A fish will make noises to keep the shoal (the group) together or to scatter them when there is danger. Fish also communicate by sending vibrations through the water.

Scent signals

Many other animals rely on scent signals and their sense of smell is much more sensitive than ours. You probably know that dogs can be trained to use their sense of smell for tracking down people or objects. Badgers and foxes sprinkle their territory with urine as a way of keeping in touch with each other and as a warning to other animals to keep away. Your dog is doing the same thing when he stops at every lamp post when you are taking him for a walk!

Moths and butterflies also use scent to communicate; the male can pick up the scent of a female from over a mile away, the silk moth from up to seven miles.

Ants, too, have a very sensitive sense of smell. When an ant finds a good source of food – perhaps your picnic! – it will fill its stomach, then return to the nest following the trail of *formic acid* it left on its way to the food; this may be quite a roundabout route. It will feed the other ants mouth-to-mouth and they will then follow it back to the food, all following the first scent trail. An ant can recognise ants from its own nest by their scent and it will drive out intruders.

Sight signals

Humans are not the only animals to use the expression on their faces to communicate. We may pout when we are sulking but a chimpanzee pouts when it is curious about something and laughs when it is angry or unhappy.

Wolves hunt in packs and need to co-operate to survive, so they cannot afford to fight one another. Instead they growl at each other in a *threat display* until the weaker one submits, using its ears, tail and face to show that it has given in. It will even lie down and offer its throat to the stronger wolf and the fighting will stop at once.

Cats have 'staring matches' too and dog fights are rarely as dangerous as they seem; what looks like fighting is mostly threat display.

Cats and dogs use their ears and mouth to show how they are feeling. If your dog is angry he will bare his teeth threateningly and perhaps snarl. If he is frightened he will *cower* with his tail between his legs. What sound does he make?

Insects, including moths and butterflies, are often very brightly coloured, not only to attract one another but also as a warning that they are poisonous; when a bird has eaten one and felt very ill afterwards it will remember next time it sees one and leave that particular kind alone. Some poisonous frogs have very bright colours for the same reason.

The 'eyes' on some butterflies' wings are also a means of protection; if the butterfly is about to be eaten by a bird it may open its wings wide to display the 'eyes'. The bird will be so surprised, perhaps mistaking the eyes for those of a cat, that it will give the butterfly time to get away!

One of the most interesting and mysterious creatures to use sight signals is the honey bee, which *dances*. When the bee has found a good source of food she returns to the hive to tell the others. If the food is nearby she flies in a circle, clockwise then anti-clockwise, while the other bees crowd round her, watching. If the food is further away, she can tell the others the exact spot by doing a *waggle* or *figure-of-eight* dance. The angle of the dance in relation to the sun tells the other bees the exact direction in which to fly; they have an in-built 'compass'. The further away the food is, the slower the dance. Try demonstrating to a friend where something is by dancing. It isn't easy!

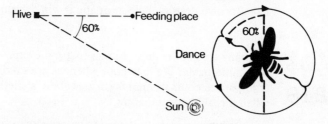

Touch signals

Chimpanzees show friendship by *grooming* one another, that is, cleaning one another's fur. They will do this whether or not they are dirty. It is rather like us talking about the weather; we have nothing important to say, perhaps, but we want to show friendship. Do you ever use language in this way?

S As we have seen, animals communicate through sound, scent, sight and touch signals. Find examples of each of these methods of communication – including some you have not read about here.

Quiz

S Now, to find out how much you know, see how many of these questions you can answer:
1. How do ants recognise each other?
2. How do chimps show friendship?
3. How does a chimp feel when it seems to be laughing?
4. Why do hens cluck all the time?
5. Why do some butterflies and moths have such bright colours?
6. What might make a male silk moth fly up to seven miles?
7. How do fish communicate?
8. How can a wolf stop a quarrel?
9. What is a *waggle dance*?
10. Why do birds sing?

| S | P | G |

Collect pictures, or draw them, for a wall display on how animals communicate. Write a few lines about each animal illustrated.

| S | P |

If you are interested in animal communication try to find out more about it; you may like to begin a project on some of the more unusual ways in which animals communicate. For example, find out about which animals use *light* to communicate, or *ultrasonic waves*. Ants, bees and insects in general also make particularly interesting subjects.

| S |

If you have a pet or if there is an animal at school, observe it as much as you can and make a list of the different ways in which it communicates, either with you or with other animals.

Questions

| G |

Now you know something about how animals communicate, compare animal language with human language by trying to find an answer to these questions. Answer each one (a) for animals and (b) for humans.

1 How do they know how to communicate?
2 Do animals/people in different countries have different languages?
3 Can they communicate about things that are far away? Can they talk about things that they cannot see, smell or hear?
4 Can animals/people talk about what happened yesterday or last year (the past) or what will happen tomorrow or next year (the future)?
5 Does the language of an animal/a person ever change? Can new ways of sending messages be found?
6 What do animals/humans communicate about?

Have you come to any conclusions about what is special about human language? If so, write them down.

Can animals talk?

People have always liked to imagine animals that could speak our language. Perhaps you can think of some animals in stories and cartoons which can talk. Is it really possible, though, for animals to talk? Parrots are very good *mimics*. They can imitate sounds perfectly, including the human voice, but to use language we need to *understand* what we are saying, and in fact parrots are not able to do this.

Some animals, including dogs and many circus animals, are intelligent enough to be trained to *obey* certain commands. Again, this is not the same as using language and in any case it is our *tone* of voice which is more important than the actual words. If you say to your dog gently, 'You nasty, dirty, ugly animal!' he will probably roll over to be tickled. If you shout angrily, 'Good dog!' he will run

5

away with his tail between his legs! Dogs are very intelligent and their sense of smell is far more sensitive than our own, but they do not seem able to use our language.

Chimpanzees are nearer to humans in intelligence. In 1947, an American couple adopted a baby chimp called Viki. They hoped that if they brought her up as their own daughter she would learn to talk. They did not succeed; after six years, although she understood a great deal, the only words she could *say* were *mama, papa, cup* and *up*. It was thought that chimps simply were not clever enough to learn human language.

More

Then in the 1960s another American couple, Allen and Beatrice Gardner, decided to try a different experiment. They knew that chimps in the wild use *sight* signals more than sound, and they had noticed from a film of Viki that she made a large number of *signs* although she did not speak. They wondered if chimps were unable simply to make the *sounds* of human speech, and they decided to teach a chimp called *Washoe* the sign language used by deaf people in America, *American Sign Language*. (You can find out about British Sign Language on page 15.)

Book

The experiment was a big success. Washoe learnt very quickly to communicate at a simple level. Her first sign was 'more!', and from the age of ten months she began to make simple sentences by using two or more signs together. She could sign 'give me a sweet' or 'you tickle me!' and even 'you me go out, hurry!' She even invented some signs of her own and taught signs to other chimps.

Since then there have been many other experiments. Another chimp called Sarah was taught to communicate using plastic shapes as symbols for words, and a gorilla called Koko learnt, like Washoe, to use sign language. She learnt to understand mention of the past and the future and she even made jokes and made up her own swear words to insult people. Once she was so cross with her teacher that she called her a 'dirty, bad toilet'! It used to be thought that humans were the only animals capable of lying but Koko even learnt to tell lie

Ball

Many people believe that human language began as sign language. So far, the animals have been able to communicate at a very simple level only, rather like very young children learning to speak. Still, until recently, it was not thought possible for them to communicate with humans at all.

If *you* were able to communicate with animals what would you want to talk about? Remember that their world is very different from our own.

Human communication without words

We often forget that words are not the only way humans communicate. We too use sound, scent, sight and touch signals.

Sound signals:
The *way* we say something (our tone of voice) can be more important than *what* we say and we often use sounds, not words, to show our feelings. For example, what sound might you make if you were (a) surprised? (b) disappointed? (c) relieved? (d) in pain?

Scent signals:
We are less aware of this but people do use aftershave and perfume to make themselves more attractive.

Sight signals:
These are the signals we are going to look at in the most detail . . .

Face talk

S P

1. Experiment by 'making faces' to see how many parts of your face you can move. How do you feel when you raise your eyebrows, wrinkle your nose or turn down the corners of your mouth?
2. Make a list of what your face can communicate.

You have probably made a list of feelings or *emotions*. As you will have discovered, humans have very *mobile* faces and we can show our feelings by moving the different parts of our face. Often our face is a better guide to how we feel than the words we use.

Study these pictures and say what you think each person was feeling when the photographs were taken.

G The Emotion Game

To play this game you will need to make a pack of eight small cards for each group of three or four. On each card write one of these words:

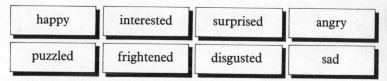

| happy | interested | surprised | angry |
| puzzled | frightened | disgusted | sad |

Each player begins the game with 10 points.
1. Shuffle the cards and place them face down in the middle.
2. Player number 1 takes the top card and has to 'act out' the word written on it.
3. The other players must guess what the word is. If someone guesses correctly, that person and the 'actor' each gain a point. If the person is wrong they both lose 2 points. If no-one has guessed after two turns then the card goes back into the pack and player number 2 takes a card. The winner is the person with the most points when everyone has had two turns.

Which parts of your face seemed to express each emotion?

Is the expression on our face usually as noticeable as you were making it in the game or did you have to exaggerate to make it easier to guess?

'Putting on' faces

When you were playing the 'Emotion Game' did you find it easy to guess which feelings were being expressed? Were some easier to act than others? If we can 'put on' faces do you think they are always such a reliable guide to our feelings? In fact we learn from quite an early age to hide our feelings by *controlling* the look on our face, perhaps to be polite or to avoid hurting people. Have you ever had to pretend you were pleased when really you were very disappointed? Are you good at hiding your feelings? Would you prefer it if people always showed what they were thinking?

Sometimes we put a particular expression on our face to send a message which may be quite different from the message in our words. (The tone of our voice helps too.)

For example:
1. We might say we don't mind about something – but make it clear we are disappointed or annoyed by the expression on our face – so the person we are talking to can't fail to know how we feel. Have you ever done this?

8

NO MATHS TEST!
WHAT A SHAME!

2. We might say something but make it clear by our expression that our words are not to be taken seriously.

Can you think of some other examples? Draw cartoons to illustrate them.

Sometimes we do not want to communicate at all. We may not want to laugh so we keep 'a straight face'. A card player may look 'poker-faced' so that the other players cannot guess his cards.

Although people all over the world share the same range of expressions for what they are feeling, there is a great deal of difference in the *amount* of emotion they show. Japanese people, for example, try not to let their feelings show, especially if they are unhappy. In public they try to wear a *blank* face. Englishmen earlier this century were told to 'keep a stiff upper lip', that is, not to let their feelings show. Boys are often taught that it is babyish to cry, and it is unusual in Britain nowadays to see men crying even when they are very upset although it has not always been so. In many other countries it is normal for women *and* men to cry and English men can seem cold-hearted! What do you think?

Body language

S

Have you ever been able to sense the mood someone was in without knowing what was giving it away? We sometimes say we can feel 'an atmosphere' which tells us that someone is in a bad mood or that two people have just had a quarrel. Without realising it they are sending us signals and we are receiving them. These signals are sometimes called 'body language'; our mood may be communicated by the way we stand, sit or walk. For example how do you think these people feel about each other?

9

G The Mood Game

Try another acting game. This time you will need a mask (a paper bag with holes cut out for the eyes will do) and one set of ten cards for the whole class, each card with one of these words written on it:

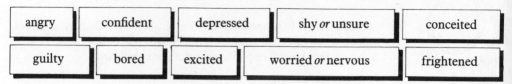

| angry | confident | depressed | shy *or* unsure | conceited |
| guilty | bored | excited | worried *or* nervous | frightened |

1. A member of the class takes the mask and a card and leaves the room.
2. The person comes back in wearing the mask and has to 'tell' the class what is on the card from the way he/she comes into the room and sits down. The class must guess what was written on the card and then work out what gave it away, or why it was hard to guess.
3. The card now goes back into the pack and the person who guessed correctly takes a card.

We often come to conclusions about what people are like from the way they stand or walk. Why do you think soldiers are made to stand up straight? Why are schoolchildren often told to 'sit up'?

Eye talk

Our eyes are said to be our most expressive feature, that is, they communicate more than any other part of our face.

Can you tell what this person is feeling from her eyes?

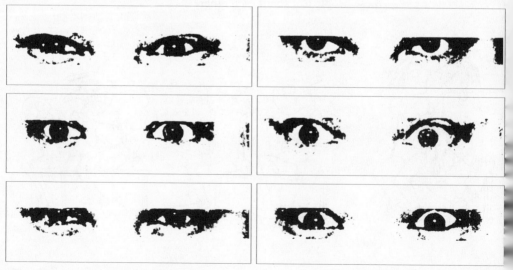

Because our eyes can communicate so much, it is sometimes said that a 'steady gaze' means honesty; the person has nothing to hide. When we are not telling the truth we may find it hard to look at the person we are talking to; what do we mean if we say a person is 'shifty'? However, when two people are in conversation it is still very unlikely that they will look at each other all the time unless they are deeply in love! Have you ever had a staring match? Try having one now! It is surprisingly difficult to hold someone's gaze for long. Like many animals we start to feel very uncomfortable when we are being stared at, and we want to look away.

When we are talking to people we seem to follow certain rules about eye contact (looking and looking away).

Watch people in conversation to see whether they look at each other more when listening or speaking. Do some people seem to use more eye contact than others?

Territory

We even use the space around us as a way of sending messages about ourselves. Like animals, people seem to need a certain amount of space, and our *privacy* is very important to us. In big cities where there is overcrowding, people may not be able to have enough space to themselves and they may react by being more unfriendly or aggressive than people in less crowded areas.

At home you probably have an area which you feel is yours. If someone moves your things, perhaps to tidy up, you may even feel annoyed. Just as some animals mark their territory with a scent trail, we mark ours with objects, pictures and posters so that we feel 'at home'. How do you like to mark out your territory?

Even when we are away from home we often claim a territory; do you have a particular place for each lesson? How do you feel when someone else sits there? On a train we may mark 'our place' with a coat or a bag, and on the beach with a towel. We feel very cross if anyone comes too close!

Even when we are walking about we seem to carry an invisible space with us which we don't like anyone to cross. Have you ever felt uncomfortable because the person you were talking too was too close?

P Find out what your 'personal space' is by measuring the distance at which it feels comfortable for you to be standing talking to someone. Is it the same for everyone in the class? Try moving closer to people as you are talking to them and see if they move back.

Experiments have shown that some people like to have more space than others. In Mediterranean countries such as Greece and Italy, people like to keep each other at 'elbow length'. For the English the distance is greater, more like arm's length. Do you agree? People from different countries may be thought 'pushy' or 'stand-offish' simply because they have different 'personal spaces'. Imagine a conversation between an Italian and an English person, both trying to establish the right distance between each other!

Gesture

Although we are not normally aware of it, most of us use our hands when we are talking. You can see this by turning down the sound on your television set. Notice how much the speakers use their hands as they talk. Our hands can show the shape and size of things (try describing a spiral staircase without using your hands!) and *emphasise* what we are saying. Some gestures, though, have special meanings; what do these people seem to be saying?

These gestures are not made naturally: we have to learn them and they vary from one country to another. For example, how do you call someone to you? In Spain and many other countries you *beckon* someone with your palm *down*, which can look like the English sign for sending someone away. In Italy you wave good-bye with the *back* of your hand which can look the English sign for beckoning someone!

What do you mean when you nod or shake your head? Nodding seems to be one of the few gestures found in nearly every country; it seems to mean 'yes' almost everywhere but in some parts of India, for example, *shaking* the head *also* means 'yes'. In Greece and Southern Italy and many other parts of the world, throwing the head back, which can look like a nod, means 'no'.

When you see your friends, how do you greet them? People in many countries find the English cold and unfriendly because they often do no more than say 'hello'. Even adults shake hands usually only the first time they meet. French people, including schoolchildren, shake hands with their friends, or kiss them on both cheeks if they are close friends, each time they meet and when they leave one another. At home they do not go to bed without kissing everyone in the family good night, on both cheeks, and shaking hands with any visitors. The same thing happens in the morning. How do you think a French child might feel staying in your family?

Other countries have different ways of greeting. The Eskimos rub noses. In Samoa people sniff one another and in Polynesia you take hold of your friend's hands and use them to stroke your face. In Tibet it is very polite to stick your tongue out at someone; you are saying 'there is no evil thought on my tongue'!

In some parts of East Africa it is considered very unlucky to point with your fingers and so people turn their heads and pout their lips in the direction they mean. In Britain some people 'cross their fingers' for good luck but in Austria and Germany they hold their thumbs. In Britain, if the people in an audience do not like a performer and if they are not very polite they may clap their hands slowly to mean 'go away!'. In other parts of Europe the slow hand clap is a great compliment! In Britain people may stand up as a sign of respect. In some other countries they sit down to show that they look *up* to the person.

There are many other signs used in different countries, and what is an insult in one country may not be understood or may have quite a different meaning in another. The English do not use gesture as much as many other people and it is very easy for misunderstandings to arise.

S   Try to spot six different gestures between now and your next lesson. Watch your friends, teachers, family, and people on television or in the street. Draw some of the gestures and say why you think they were used.

Miming

Have you ever tried to manage without speech altogether? It is surprising how much we can communicate when we have to, through mime and gesture. Imagine yourself in a country where you cannot use speech because you have no language in common with the people who live there. What would you need to be able to communicate? How would you go about it?

You could probably survive at least by pointing, miming and drawing pictures. Which words do you think it would be most useful to learn first?

P Now imagine that no-one in your class can speak or write. Work out with a friend how you could communicate these messages. (Some will be easier than others.)

1. Which is the way to the station, please?
2. I'm hungry! I'd like some chicken and chips!
3. How far is it to the swimming pool?
4. What time is it?
5. I think Maths is easy!
6. School is cancelled this afternoon!

Were there any messages you couldn't communicate? What made some of them harder than others?

P With a friend prepare a simple message to be communicated to the rest of the class. (Ask your teacher for ideas if you are stuck.) Remember that you are communicating to people who do not speak English! There is no need to mime every word; you should try to communicate the *idea* behind the message.

Do you think miming is a very effective method of communication? What are the advantages? What are the problems?

You have probably decided that miming can be very useful when people cannot speak to one another. You may also have found that it is very easy to *mis*understand and it can take a long time to deliver the message. Unlike speech, mime usually needs the full attention of the sender and the receiver and, of course, you need to be able to see one another.

G

When we mime we are acting out or making pictures of what we want to say. That is why we can mime only quite simple messages. Try holding a class discussion on whether or not school uniform is a good thing. You may have very strong views but you will probably be unable to express them in mime; it is very difficult to mime ideas.

How can deaf people communicate?

As they are unable to hear, deaf people use *sight* for communication. They may learn to lip-read in order to communicate with hearing people, but a far more effective means of communication is sign language.

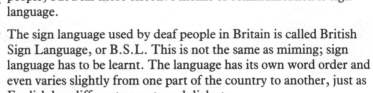

The sign language used by deaf people in Britain is called British Sign Language, or B.S.L. This is not the same as miming; sign language has to be learnt. The language has its own word order and even varies slightly from one part of the country to another, just as English has different accents and dialects.

In spoken English some words are 'sound pictures'; words like *slap* or *crash* or *whisper* or *hum* sound like their meaning. Perhaps you can think of some others? Most words sound nothing like their meaning, though; the word 'bird' does not sound like a bird and we might just as easily call it 'Vogel' as in German or 'oiseau' as in French or 'pájaro' as in Spanish.

In the same way, in B.S.L. some words *look* like their meaning; the word for 'shoe' for example is made by miming putting on a shoe, but most words have little or nothing to do with their meaning and have to be learnt.

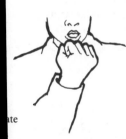

Not only do deaf people use their hands to communicate, they also use their faces, including their eyes, the shape of their lips, and their whole body. All this makes it quite a difficult language to learn to use well!

Using sign language, deaf people can discuss feelings and ideas, argue, joke, communicate with one another as effectively in fact as hearing people. The disadvantage is that the language is understood by so few hearing people.

There is an alphabet which can be used to spell out English words but this can be quite slow. B.S.L. is much quicker and deaf people who use it can communicate as quickly as hearing people.

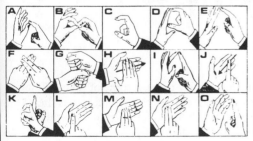
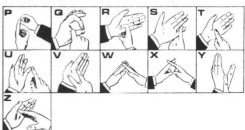

Manual alphabet

15

3 Signals and signs

Signals

People have always needed to communicate quickly over long distances, and before the invention of the telegraph and telephone other ways had to be found. Messengers could be sent but they could not always travel fast enough. The American Indians used smoke signals; what kind of messages do you think they needed to send? In some parts of Africa drums were used to send messages; the sound could travel up to twenty miles. In the army, movements are timed with a drum on the parade ground as they once were in battle. In England a system of bonfires or *beacons* was used to spread news very quickly; when the Spanish Armada approached in 1588 beacons were lit all over the country. This tradition still survives today to celebrate state occasions. For example a beacon was lit by Prince Charles on the eve of his wedding in July 1981.

In the eighteenth century *semaphore* was developed as a signalling system for use on ships and, later, the railway. It was used a great deal, before the invention of radio. Messages could be read from miles away and sent on to people at the next semaphore post. To signal with it you need two boards on poles, two lights, two flags or two arms!

Ready A B C D E F G H I J K L M N

O P Q R S T U V W X Y Z Direction sign

P Practise making all the signals and try to learn some of them. When you have the chance, try sending messages to a friend across the school field or playground. You will find it a rather slow method of communicating until you have had plenty of practice!

16

The Morse code

When the electric telegraph was invented, in 1837, communication over long distances became easier. Samuel Morse invented an alphabet code in which the electricity was switched on and off. Switched on for a short while it gave a short click in the telegraph wire which could be written as a dot. Left for longer there was a longer 'buzz', written as a dash. Each letter of the alphabet had a different signal.

A = ·−	G = −−·	L = ·−··	Q = −−·−	V = ···−
B = −···	H = ····	M = −−	R = ·−·	W = ·−−
C = −·−·	I = ··	N = −·	S = ···	X = −··−
D = −··	J = ·−−−	O = −−−	T = −	Y = −·−−
E = ·	K = −·−	P = ·−−·	U = ··−	Z = −−··
F = ··−·				

S Now try to decode this information about Samuel Morse:

····   ·/·−−   ·−   ···/·−   −·/

·−   −−   ·   ·−·   ··   −·−·   ·−   −·/

·−−·   ·−   ··   −·   −   ·   ·−·/·−   −·   −···/

··   −·   ···−   ·   −·   −   −−−   ·−·/

P Try writing some messages in Morse Code and see if a friend can decode them. You can also send messages in Morse by shining a torch on and off.

To signal over shorter distances we may use our hands, or flashing lights, or sound. Signals may be needed because people are unable to talk. Divers, for example, have various gestures to communicate under water and there are special signals used by people working in radio or television.

Signals are used to help aircraft pilots stop in the right place and, again, the signalman uses a special code for each manoeuvre.

Diving
Let's go up

Broadcasting
Warning You are on the air
First finger draws a circle in the air, symbol for red light

Air traffic control
Start engines
Right hand draws a circle left hand points to engine

S P Here are some signals you will be more familiar with. Can you say what messages are being sent?

Signs

We also use pictures or signs to send messages, especially on the roads. The meaning of some signs is quite clear and they are used and understood all over the world.

S Here are some other signs used on the road as part of the *Highway Code*. Test your knowledge of this code by writing down the messages being sent.

S P
1. Why do we use these signs instead of writing?
2. What do you think makes a good sign?
3. Could any of these be more effective, do you think? If so how?

S P Now, perhaps with a friend, design some signs of your own. You may like to hold a class competition to see who can design the best signs. Remember that to be effective your signs must be understood at a glance by someone who cannot read English. Here are some suggestions:
1. Danger! (to stop people walking too near the edge of a cliff)
2. This is *not* drinking water! (over a tap)
3. Now wash your hands! (in a toilet)
4. Drive on the left! (on the road out from a car ferry bringing visitors from abroad)

|S| |P| Now make a list of signs which it might be useful to have in public places: at a football ground, for example, or in a department store or supermarket.

|S| Make a list of up to five different signs you see on your journey home from school. Draw them and say why they are used.

Reading a map

You will need a map for this section. Not all signs have a meaning which is obvious, some have to be learnt. Here are some signs used in maps.

|S| |P| 1. Do you know or can you guess the meaning of any of them?
2. Find out if you are right by looking at the key to the map.
3. Now you know what they mean can you see a connection between the signs and their meaning?
4. Now find out the signs used for the following.

5. Study a map of the area around your school. Trace your route home.
6. Draw a map or plan of your own of your school and its grounds or of the area where you live, using colour if possible. Put in your own symbols and provide a key.

19

 # Symbols

We communicate not only through signs but also through *symbols*. What is the difference between a sign and a symbol? The signs we have been looking at in Units 2 and 3 (and road signs, map signs and *some* signs like 'shoe' in sign language for deaf people) mostly *look* in some way like what they represent. But symbols don't have to. Their meaning has to be learnt.

S P Here are some well-known symbols. What do they mean to you?

Symbols often represent not just one thing but a whole set of ideas. They may represent a particular religion or a set of political beliefs

Sometimes colour is used in a symbolic way. For example, what colours are used to represent the different political parties in Britain?

Business companies often choose a symbol to represent their product, to mark them out from their competitors. You will find one on the back of this book. Here are some others:

These symbols are sometimes known as *logos*.

S P Imagine you have been asked by one of the following manufacturers to design a *logo* for its products:

> *TOTTERS:* children's clothing
> *LINECRAFT:* modern furniture
> *FUNTOYS:* children's toys and games
> *P.R. JONES:* expensive chocolates and sweets

20

Flags

Each country has its own flag, which can become a very powerful symbol. What different things do you think a flag might come to represent for the people of a country?

The colours are sometimes chosen because of what they represent. For example, the flag of the Bahamas is yellow for the golden sands, blue for the sea and black for the people who live there. The flag may have an *emblem* (a symbol) which says something about the country, such as a sun. Other popular emblems are crosses and stars. Draw and colour five different national flags and try to find out something about their origin.

S P G

Flags do not always represent countries. They may be the badge of an organisation such as the Red Cross (in the margin), or they may be used to signal messages. This blue and white flag (below) is called the 'Blue Peter'. Do you know what it means?

WHITE

BLUE

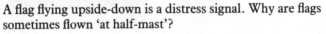

A flag flying upside-down is a distress signal. Why are flags sometimes flown 'at half-mast'?

Many national flags originated in battle; they were a symbol of the cause or country being fought for and they kept the soldiers together. In the same way, many organisations use a flag, badge, banner or colours as a symbol of what keeps their members together. Can you think of some examples? Perhaps you belong to one? You may support a football team and sometimes wear a scarf or a badge with your team's colours. Most of us are proud to belong to a particular organisation or group of people with similar interests to our own. We may even feel superior to those outside it, whether the group is our own circle of friends, a football team, a club or a political organisation. Sometimes feeling part of a group makes us forget what we consider important when we are on our own and we may find ourselves being cruel or even violent to those who are not part of our group. Has this ever happened to you?

Flags, banners and other symbols can be an important reminder to us of what we consider important. Sometimes, though, we may use them as an excuse to behave irresponsibly and to avoid thinking for ourselves.

G

Draw or make a list of 10 different badges, colours or uniforms worn by members of your class outside school. What do they represent?

Clothes

S P

The clothes we wear can be a means of communication. What are these people saying by what they are wearing? Why do they all need to wear a uniform?

S P G

Many British schoolchildren wear a uniform. Perhaps you do? Do you think it is a good idea? Make a list of the arguments for and against school uniform.

Whether we are in uniform or not, the clothes we wear and the way we wear them send messages about the sort of person we are or would like to be. We often think we know what people are like, the sort of job they do and even how much money they have because of the clothes they are wearing. Are we always right?

Even in jobs where people do not have a uniform they are often expected to dress in a particular way. We all wear different clothes for different occasions and the clothes we wear can affect the way we feel. Do you think they can even affect our behaviour? If so, how?

What about you?

Try to find an answer to these questions:
1. Are clothes important to you? Why?
2. Do you always choose the clothes you wear? How do you decide what to wear?
3. Think of three occasions for which you would dress differently.
4. Which clothes do you feel most comfortable in? Why?
5. Do you like to be fashionable? Why?
6. Do you ever criticise people for the way they are dressed? If so, why?
7. How do you expect your teachers to dress? Do you think they should wear a uniform?
8. Do you think your teachers dress differently when they are not at school? Try to find out.
9. Find out what your parents and grandparents wore when they were at school. Are they in favour of school uniform? Why?
10. Find out what was fashionable when your parents and grandparents were young. How many different fashions have they seen?

11. Where do fashions come from? Who decides what is fashionable and how do people know what the latest fashions are?
12. Why do you think fashions change so very quickly?

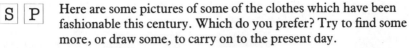

Here are some pictures of some of the clothes which have been fashionable this century. Which do you prefer? Try to find some more, or draw some, to carry on to the present day.

1920   1940   1960   1980

Unisex

Do you think men and women ought to dress differently? We even have special colours for babies: blue for boys, pink for girls. What do these colours make you think of? Do you think they say something about how we expect the children to grow up?

We often expect women to dress more colourfully than men and to pay more attention to their appearance. Why do you think this is? In Britain in the early 19th century it was the men who dressed up and took most care over their appearance and this is so today in many parts of the world.

Find out how men and women's fashions have changed over the centuries. Try to find out some of the reasons for the changing fashions.

The language of heraldry

Just as in sport the teams wear colours in order to be recognised easily, so, in the 12th century, knights wore brightly-coloured coats called *coats-of-arms* over their armour so they could be easily identified. Each rich family had its own coat-of-arms, that is, its own colours and pattern, which might be chosen because it looked attractive or because it showed something about the knight's way of life, achievements or ambitions. Sometimes there might be a *pun* on the family name (for example, the Trumpingtons' coat of arms showed trumpets). It could be divided into four (quartered) to show parts of other coats-of-arms, and added to. Coats-of-arms became so complicated that a special language was built up to describe them. Describing a coat-of-arms is known as *blazoning*.

23

Coat-of-arms of Cambridge University

Here are some of the colours used in heraldry.

Metals: or (gold or yellow) *argent* (silver or white).
Colours: azure (blue) *gules* (red) *vert* (green) *sable* (black).

In the illustration, you can see some of the patterns used. They are called *ordinaries*.

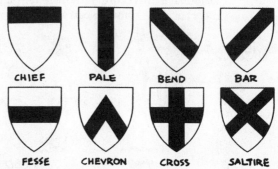

CHIEF   PALE   BEND   BAR

FESSE   CHEVRON   CROSS   SALTIRE

Onto these designs was often added a *charge* (an emblem or symbol) such as an animal, a bird, a flower, a shell or a leaf.

In the language of heraldry, when you are describing a coat-of-arms (blazoning), you name the background colour first (the *field*) then the main pattern (the *ordinary*) and its colour, then any other patterns (*charges*) and their colours.

For example, a shield with a red background and a gold bar across can be described, 'gules a fesse or'. Now draw and colour these shields.

1. Argent a chevron azure   3. Gules a pale or
2. Or a bend vert   4. Argent a cross gules

One of the rules of heraldry is that a metal must not be placed on a metal or a colour on a colour. This is to give as much contrast as possible.

Now you know a little about heraldry, design your own coat-of-arms. Keep to the basic designs (ordinaries) but use your own *emblems*. If you are good at running, for example, you might include a pair of running shoes in one quarter, or you might choose an animal which runs fast. If your favourite colour is blue then azure may form the background to your shield. Make your shield as attractive and as imaginative as you can (the most effective ones are fairly simple) and make sure it says something about *you*.

Does your school have a crest or coat-of-arms? If so, try to find out where it came from. Look out for coats-of-arms in churches, on town halls, in banks and other organisations.

Made-up languages

5

Music

S P

As far as we know, music has always been an important means of communication and it would be hard to imagine a world without music and rhythm. We may play, sing or listen to music to suit a particular mood we are in or even to change our mood if we need 'cheering up'.

We also use music for special purposes. Can you say what the following can communicate? – a lullaby – an ice cream van tune – a hymn – the music at the start of a television programme – a national anthem. Can you add to this list?

For a very long time music was not written down but was passed on from person to person and from generation to generation. Over the centuries a system of symbols has developed so that a composer can now set down on paper exactly what she or he has in mind for someone else to sing or play, just as an author can write a book for others to read. The writing down of music is called *notation* and, like other *symbolic* languages, it has to be learnt.

The tune: The way the notes rise and fall is shown by making marks on the lines and the spaces between the lines of a *stave*. Ask someone in your class with a recorder or another musical instrument to play these notes, and follow them on the stave.

Rhythm: Most music has some kind of a regular beat or *rhythm*. It is what makes us tap our feet when we are listening to something lively. We can show the rhythm of a tune by putting a line in front of each note to be *stressed*.

Try clapping each of these rhythms.

25

Now choose just one of the rhythms and see if someone else can guess which one you are clapping.

The length of the notes: We also need to know how long each note will last:

♩   *one beat*

♪   *half* a beat (two together can be written like this: ♫)

𝅗𝅥   *two* beats

𝅗𝅥.   *three* beats

𝅝   *four* beats

Try clapping these rhythms (it may help to count the beats out loud).

Find out from someone in the class who can read music what the different notes are called.

Of course there are all sorts of other symbols used in music, and even words to show how it is to be played or sung. These words are mostly Italian. Here are some of them; try to find out what they mean:

allegro forte piano andante crescendo staccato

Finally, sing this song, following the music:

Hap-py birth-day to you Hap-py birth-day to you Hap-py birth-day dear   Fred,   Happy birth-day to   you!

Dance

Dance is another of the oldest forms of communication and each country has its own folk dances, some of which can be very difficult to learn; in some Indian dances the movement even of a finger can have a special meaning and a dance can tell a very complicated story.

Make a list of some other kinds of dance and say where they might be performed.

Dances are usually simply handed on from one person to another (as music used to be); it seems as hard to capture a dance on paper as to capture music. It can be done though and a *choreographer* (someone who arranges a dance) can set out a whole ballet on paper. There are symbols for each part of the body and their position, movement and the rhythm is shown, like music, on a stave.

Look at the illustrations. They show the two most common ways of writing dance and, although they may look very confusing, they are learnt and understood by many dancers today. Like other made-up languages they make sense only to those people who have learnt them.

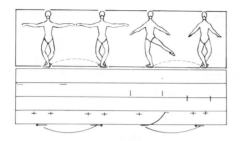

Labanotation   Benesh dance notation

Numbers

Mathematics has a language of its own using numbers and often replacing words with symbols; what do all the symbols *mean* in the sum, $2 \times 2 + 2 - 2 \div 2 = ?$ What is the answer? Numbers themselves are only symbols and the numbering system we use is not the only one possible; perhaps you have come across Roman numerals where these symbols are used? L(50) C(100) D(500) M(1,000). Numbers 1 – 10 are written like this: I, II, III, IV, V, VI, VII, VIII, IX, X.

S P Find out what these numbers are: XII, XV, XXX, XXXXIII, LXXII, MMCLXXXIII. Which system do you prefer? Why?

Algebra

For complicated mathematical calculations there is a language called *algebra* which uses letters instead of numbers. For example, from this sum, $a + 6 = 9$, we can work out that a must be 3.

S P Work out what x and y represent from this information:

$x + 4 = 10$ and $y = x - 2$. What is $x + y$?

Graphs and charts

Information concerning numbers (*statistics*) can be set out in various ways. It may be set out in the form of a *table* but as tables can be difficult to read if there is a large amount of information, *graphs* are often used instead; they turn the information into a sort of picture. Here are four of the most commonly-used graphs. They are often used in newspapers and on television where information needs to be presented quickly and attractively, to make a particular point.

A line graph

Line graphs are especially useful for showing changes over a period of time. This one shows the change of temperature in a classroom.

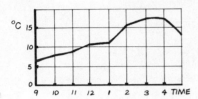

A bar chart

Bar charts are useful for comparing pieces of information. This one shows the favourite colours of the members of a class.

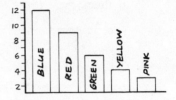

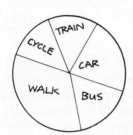

A pie chart

Pie charts are easy to read but hard to draw accurately. This one shows the means of transport used by a group of people to go to work.

A pictogram

Pictograms are often used in advertising. They are eye-catching but often inaccurate. This one shows the number of vehicles. which passed a particular spot over 15 minutes.

 P G

If the information has been collected by asking people's opinion, again we need to look very carefully. Since not everyone can be asked, has a fair sample been taken? Did everyone tell the truth and were the questions fair?

Carry out some surveys of your own and represent your findings on a graph. Here are some suggestions:

1. Carry out an opinion poll to see which television channel *or* toothpaste *or* method of travelling to school is most popular in your class. Show the results on a pie chart.
2. Find out which colour *or* school subject *or* chocolate bar *or* television programme is most popular. Show the results on a bar chart.
3. Find out which sport is most popular. Show the results on a pictogram.

Computers, codes and communication

At one time very few people knew how to read or write. They seemed to hold almost magic powers and writing seemed like a mysterious, secret code, much too complicated for ordinary people to understand. Nowadays many more people can read and write, but now it is computers and computer languages that appear (to many of us) mysterious and confusing.

Computers are used more and more for calculating and storing information, not because they can do things which humans cannot but because they work more quickly and with a greater number of figures. They have had an enormous effect on our lives and are used by almost every kind of organisation from businesses to governments. A travel agent can tell a customer immediately if there is space on a particular flight by checking into a central computer. All branches of a particular bank are linked by computer so that they can find out at once how much money a customer has in his or her account. A police officer can trace the owner of a car almost immediately by 'feeding' its registration number into a computer. There is so much information about us all stored in computers that many people worry that it may be misused. It is very important for all organisations to ensure that their information is accurate and up-to-date, and that it is available only to the right people.

Talking to a computer

A computer can only do what it is told and computer languages consist of a series of orders. To use a computer we have to be very precise in our instructions; even commas and full stops have special meanings. There is only one way to give each order and, unlike us, the computer cannot guess what is meant if the order is put differently; it simply cannot obey.

The easiest computer language, nearest to English, is called *Basic*. Here is a simple program in Basic to multiply any two numbers together, whether it is 2×2 or 3,468,294,891×1.0786420183!

Program	Meaning
10 Rem. A program to multiply 2 numbers and print the answer	'Rem.' tells the computer to do nothing! This line is only to tell the *programmer* what the program is for.
20 Print 'what is the 1st number'	The computer must print the question so the programmer knows when to type in the first number.
30 Read A	The computer must read and store the first number, calling it A.
40 Print 'what is the 2nd number' 50 Read B	The computer will read and store the second number when it is typed in, calling it B.
60 Let C=A*B	The computer must multiply the two numbers (A×B) and call the answer C.
70 Print A,'×',B,'=',C	The computer must print the first number (A) 'times' the second
80 End	number (B) 'equals' and the answer (C).

Each line has a number so the computer follows instructions in the right order. The computer will store this program until it is needed.

Because *Basic* uses so many English words it cannot deal with very complicated scientific and business information; there are other languages using words and symbols further away from English but nearer the code used in the computer, such as *Fortran, Algol* and *Cobol.*

S   Try to find out from people you know *two* different uses made of computers at work. What language do they use?

Secret codes

Sometimes people may deliberately stop others from understanding by using a signal, language or code understood only by them. At an auction a person might arrange with the auctioneer that every time he or she coughed, the bid was raised by £100. Secret societies may have a secret handshake, gesture or a written code which only the members understand.

Secret written codes are also used by governments and in the Army, Navy and Air Force; in the Navy the code book is covered in lead so that if it is likely to fall into enemy hands it can be thrown overboard and will sink to the bottom. Not all codes are secret, though; semaphore and Morse, for example, are *open* codes; they are used for convenience and anyone who wants to can find out what they mean.

Have you ever tried making up your own secret code? This one uses the position of the letters on a grid to help you remember it:

 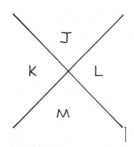 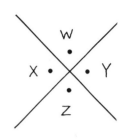

For example, here is the title of this book written in the code:

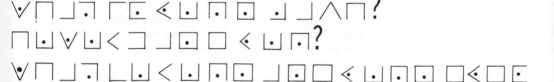

S Now try to decode these messages and answer them in the code.

With a friend, practise sending and decoding messages in this code (you can make it more secret by beginning with a different letter on the grid).

Now make up your own secret code which no-one will be able to understand.

What do you think?

Now you have worked your way through the book, here are some more difficult questions on some of the topics you have covered, to make you think about them further.

1. What would happen to the world if suddenly we all lost our ability to communicate? Make a list of the things which would change, or write a story about it.

2. Dolphins, bats and many other creatures can make and hear sounds which are *inaudible* to us because they are too high-pitched or not loud enough. Find other examples which show that some animals' *senses* are more highly-developed than our own.

3. We say that parrots cannot use human language, although they can speak, and some people believe that Washoe and Koko do use language, although they *cannot* speak. Can you explain this? What is language?

4. No-one knows how or when humans first began to use speech to communicate although there are very many theories. Have you any ideas? Discuss your theories with a group of friends or write them down.

5. How do we show our feelings to other people? Make a list of as many ways as possible.

6. Do you think gestures such as waving, shaking hands or shrugging are *instinctive* or do they have to be learnt? What evidence do you have?

7. What are the advantages of speech over other methods of communication? What are the advantages of being able to *write* language as well?

8. How do deaf people communicate? What do you think are the problems met by a deaf person living and working with hearing people?

9. Why do we use signs and symbols as well as speaking and writing? Make a list of reasons.

10. (a) Make a list of the different things *clothes* can communicate.
    (b) Why do people like to be fashionable?

11. You may have noticed that many of the words used in heraldry, to describe coats-of-arms, are *French*. Find out why this is, and also why many of the words used in music are *Italian* (e.g.